SCHIRMER'S LIBRARY
OF MUSICAL CLASSICS

Vol. 1985

Isaac Albeniz

Piano Album

ISBN 0-7935-3041-5

G. SCHIRMER, Inc.

DISTRIBUTED BY

7777 W. BLUEMOUND RD. P.O. BOX 13819 MILWAUKEE, WI 53213

CONTENTS

Clayton Bourassa : Cantos de España 12/11/06

Isaac Albéniz
(1860-1909)

Isaac Albéniz is one of Spain's most important composers and pianists. A child prodigy, he gave his first piano performance at the age of four in Barcelona and only three years later, at age seven, he began composing, writing a *Marcha militar* ("Military March") as his first work.

That same year, 1867, Albéniz was taken to Paris to study at the Conservatoire with Marmontel, the teacher of Debussy. Although his youthful pranks caused the Conservatoire to reject Albéniz as a permanent student, his parents realized the economic potential of their young son's tremendous talent and began taking him on endless concert tours. Albéniz retaliated by running away from home on numerous occasions and organizing concert tours of his own. By age twelve he traveled alone as far as Argentina, New York and San Francisco. He then returned to Europe to study with Carl Reinecke in Leipzig. Later he received a scholarship which gave him the opportunity to continue his studies at the Brussels Conservatory. Finally, he studied with Franz Liszt both in Weimar and in Rome.

Although he was a virtuoso pianist, Albéniz is primarily remembered as a composer. He was the first of the three major composers (the others being Enrique Granados and Manuel de Falla) Spain produced at the end of the Nineteenth Century. Albeniz' formal training as a composer was primarily his studies with Felip Pedrell. Pedrell is widely credited as having formed the modern Spanish school of composers. The extent of Pedrell's influence on Albéniz is difficult to judge. Certainly he outwardly incorporated Pedrell's call for Spanish nationalism into his music. Albéniz was a Romantic Nationalist inspired by the natural beauty of Spain and the vivid character of its people. He was by far the most forward looking of his colleagues, introducing some of the most advanced musical trends of his day into Spain. His extensive contacts in Paris with Ernest Chausson, Gabriel Fauré, and Vincent d'Indy influenced Albeniz strongly, without distracting him from the inspiration of his native country. Albéniz' mature music is dazzling, picturesque and thoroughly refined.

Albéniz composed five *Sonatas* for piano between 1883 and 1886. Of these works only the *Minuetto del gallo* from the fifth *Sonata* is played with any frequency today. Certainly it is one of the best movements from the *Sonatas*. Also among Albéniz' early works is *Recuerdos de viaje*. The seven pieces of the suite (*En la playa* is the final movement) are representative of the salon-style in which Albéniz wrote at the time. Music of this type was extremely popular with pianists of the day.

With *España*, *Cantos de España*, and the *Suite española* Albéniz created a new style of descriptive music, evoking the colorful rhythms and moods of different regions of Spain. Written in a more sophisticated style than his earlier works, the various movements of the suites provide a kind of postcard view of Spain. Albéniz' stylizations of Spanish traditional music and dance rhythms suffuse each of these highly colorful pieces which seduce us with exotic charm.

The suite *Iberia* is Albéniz' masterpiece, and, in addition, is one of the most original works of the piano literature. The music has a richness and density of texture which makes it extremely difficult to play. Yet, it is not merely a work of transcendental virtuosity, but a series of tone poems evoking Spain. *Iberia* was highly praised by Claude Debussy, who wrote that "never has music attained such diverse, such colored impressions; the eyes close as if dazzled by having seen too many images." *Evocación* and *El puerto* are the first two pieces of the suite and the easiest from a technical standpoint. *Evocación*, which was originally titled "Prelude", serves to evoke the essence of Spain. *El puerto* depicts the port city of El puerto de Santa María and its luminous light.

Azulejos ("Glazed Tiles") was the first of a projected suite left unfinished by Albéniz. On his deathbed he asked his close friend Enrique Granados to complete his piece. Granados' manuscript begins with measure 63 of the completed work. The 89 measures added by Granados continue *Azulejos* in the style begun by Albéniz and form a moving tribute to his friend.

In spite of the fact that he completed *Azulejos* in an entirely convincing manner, the mature Granados and his fellow Catalan shared no stylistic traits. *Iberia* and *Goyescas* are two of the major landmarks of Spanish music, written at almost the same time by Spanish composers who both studied composition with Pedrell, yet they are entirely different in their musical language, and in the impact they had on future composers. *Goyescas* brought Romanticism to a close. In *Iberia* Albéniz was strongly influenced by contemporary French music. The suite represented a new direction in Spanish music, and demanded of pianists an entirely new type of pianistic technique. Albéniz' music is neither a romantic effusion nor simply an imitation of Spanish popular music. Instead he achieved a stylization of some of the essential qualities of the music of his country.

—DOUGLAS RIVA
NEW YORK

Sonata
Minuetto del gallo

"Rooster Minuet"

Isaac Albéniz, Op. 82

España

("Spain")

Preludio

("Prelude")

Isaac Albéniz, Op.165

Tango

Isaac Albéniz, Op.165

Malagueña
("Dance from Málaga")

Isaac Albéniz, Op.165

17

Cantos de España
("Songs of Spain")
Preludio
("Prelude")

Isaac Albéniz

24

Córdoba

Isaac Albéniz

Seguidillas

Isaac Albéniz

Suite Española
("Spanish Suite")
Granada

Isaac Albéniz

Sevilla

Isaac Albéniz

MENO MOSSO

Recuerdos de viaje
("Travel Memories")
En la playa
("At the Beach")

Isaac Albéniz

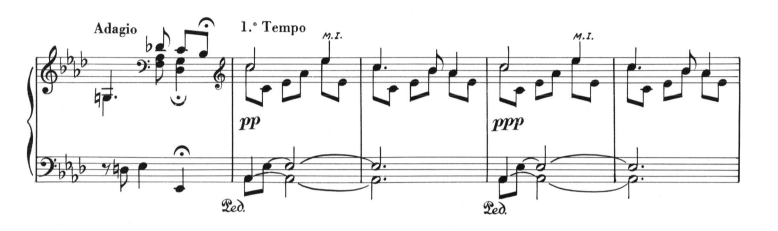

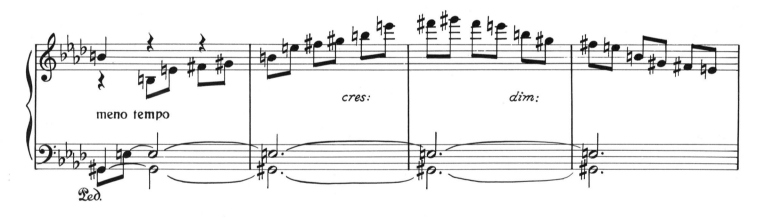

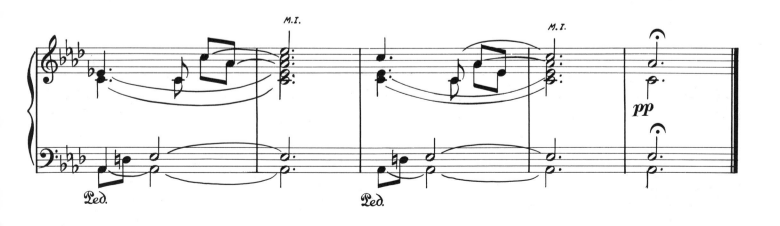

Iberia

Evocación

("Evocation")

Isaac Albéniz

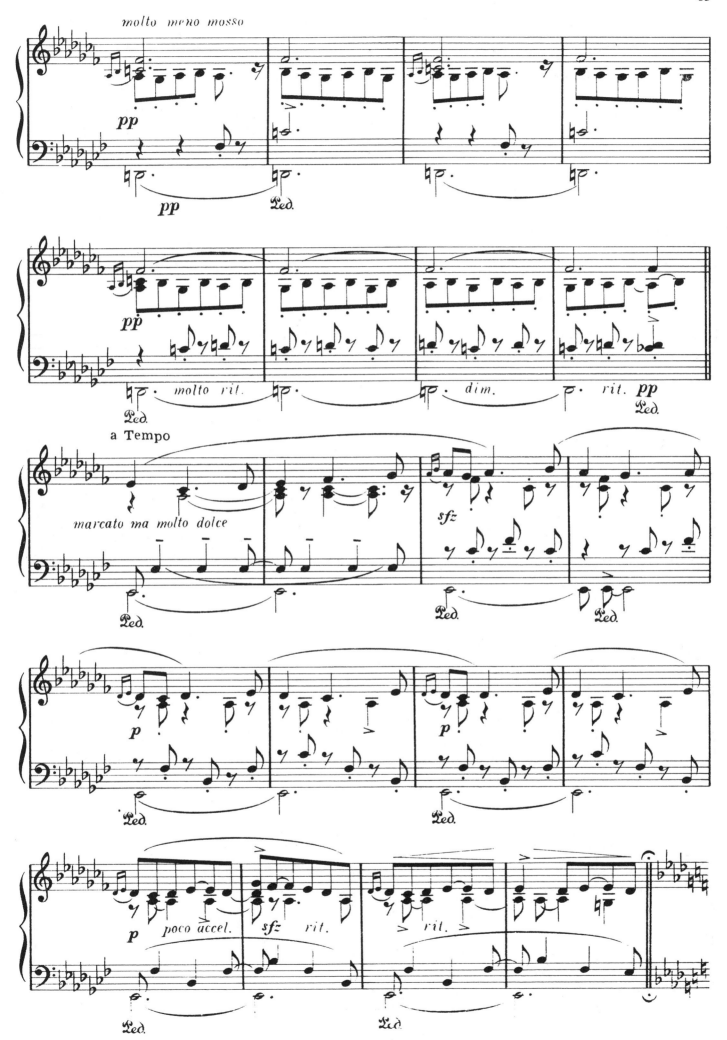

souple très doux et lointain.
meno mosso.

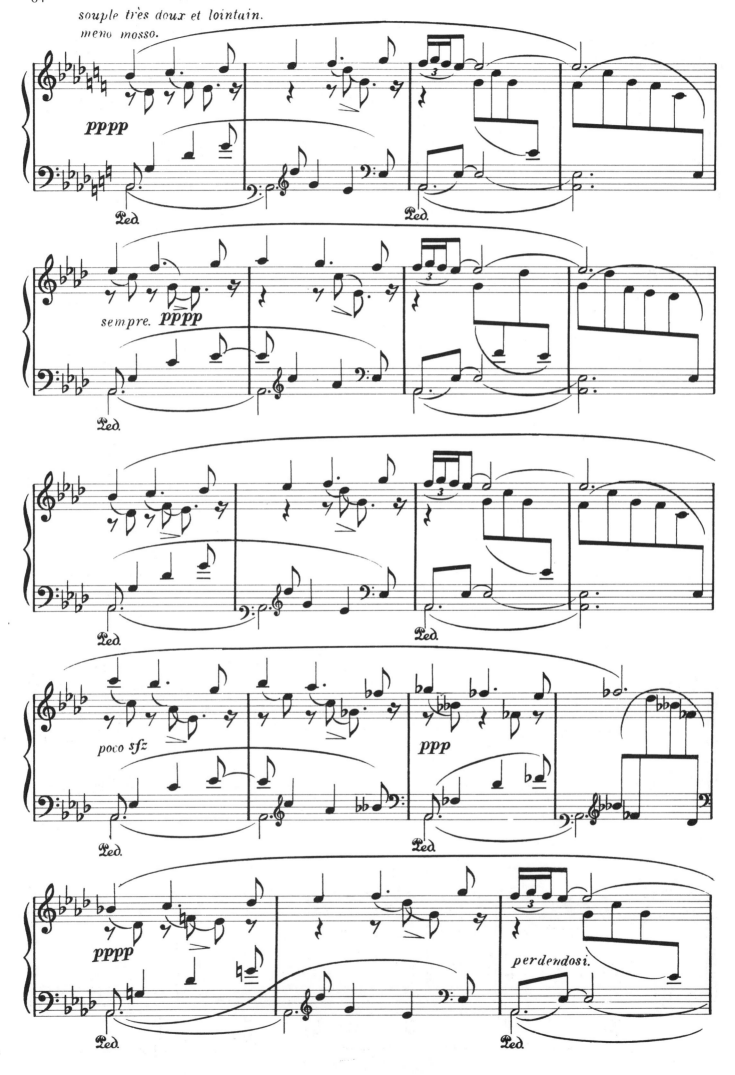

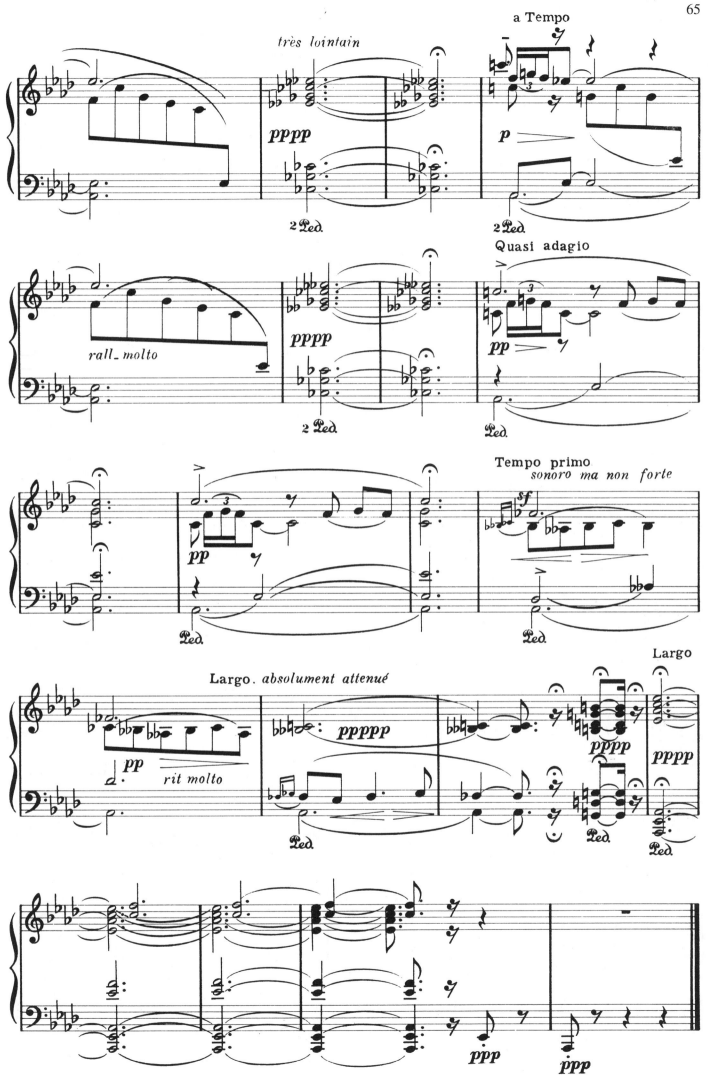

El puerto
("The Port")

Isaac Albéniz

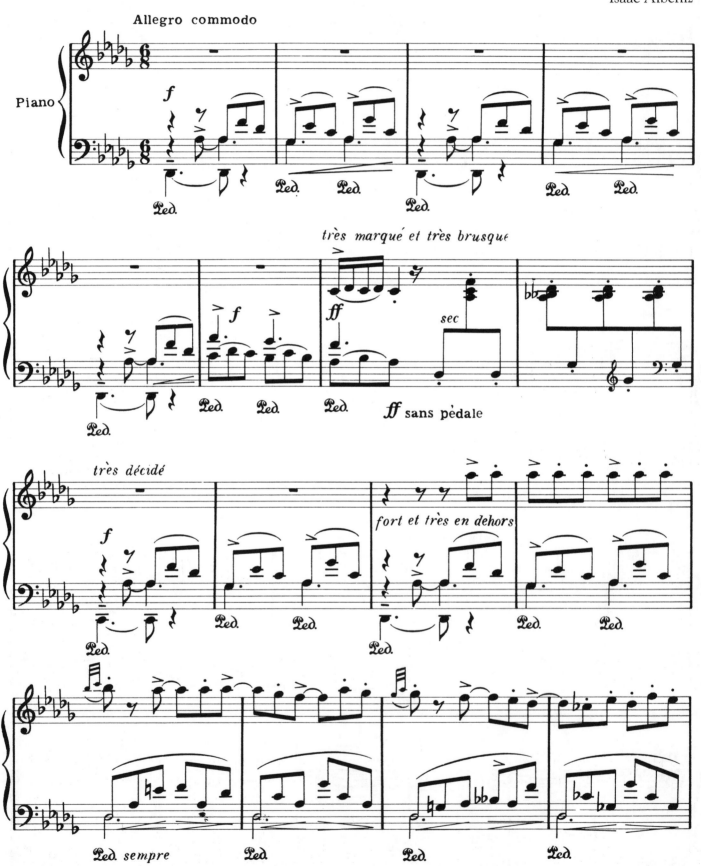

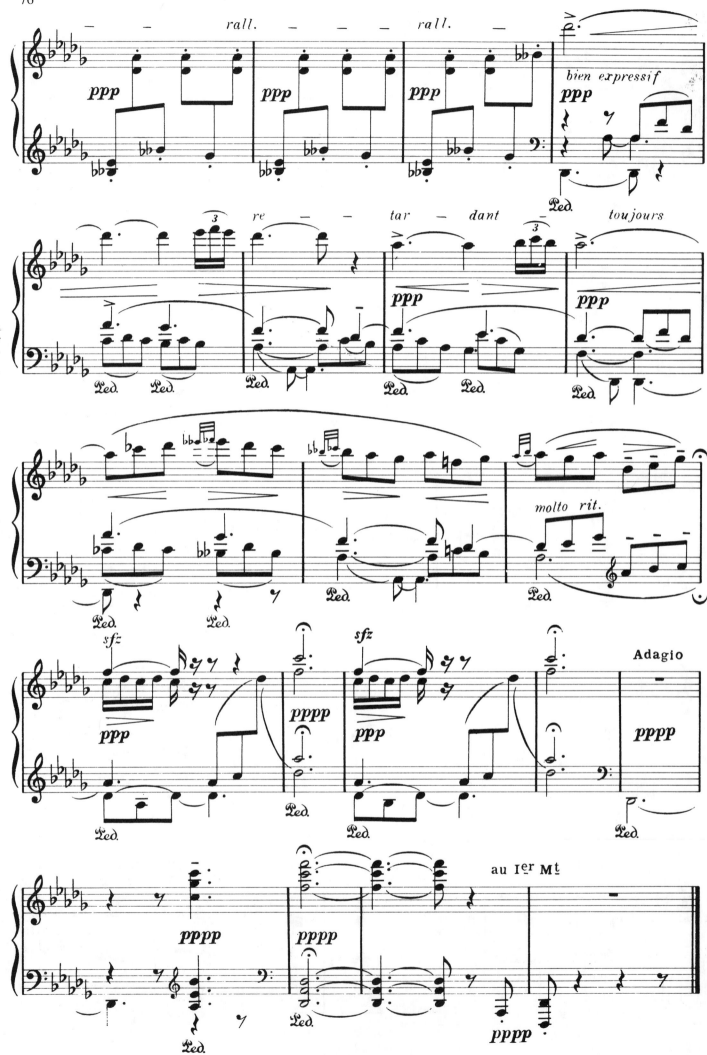

Azulejos
("Glazed Tiles")

Isaac Albéniz

completed by Enrique Granados

Appassionato